THE TABLETOP LEARNING SERIES

COOKBOOK

A No-Cook Cook & Learn Book
by Imogene Forte

Incentive Publications, Inc.
Nashville, Tennessee

Illustrated by Mary Hamilton
Cover designed by Mary Hamilton and illustrated by Jan Cunningham
Edited by Mary C. Mahoney and Susan Oglander

ISBN 0-86530-089-5
Library of Congress Catalog Number 83-80962

THIS
COOKBOOK
BELONGS TO

_____

CONTENTS

The first time you try each of these recipes,
write the date and whom you served it to on the lines below.
Then you will have a record of your cooking.

SALADS AND MAIN DISHES

DESSERTS AND SPECIAL TREATS

Using Metric Measurements

To convert the recipes in this book into metric measurements, use the following conversion chart.

VOLUME

1 teaspoon = 5 milliliters
1 tablespoon = 15 milliliters
1 fluid ounce = 30 milliliters
1 cup = 0.24 liters
1 pint = 0.47 liters
1 quart = 0.95 liters
1 gallon = 3.8 liters

MASS (WEIGHT)

1 ounce = 28 grams
1 pound = 0.45 kilograms

LENGTH

1 inch = 2.54 centimeters

A NOTE TO KIDS

Here are some steps you need to know before you begin to use this cookbook.

. . . First, the recipes are fun and easy to prepare. You can make all of them without using electrical appliances.

. . . Every recipe includes a list of ingredients and utensils to be used, plus step-by-step directions for completing it. Read the *entire* recipe before you start to cook. Then gather your materials, arrange your work space, and plan your time.

. . . Pages 73-77 contain an illustrated glossary to help you understand cooking terms and use the tools and equipment properly. Study these pages, and you will be on your way to becoming a good cook.

. . . You might need grown-up assistance when using a sharp knife or can opener, and as you read and try to understand directions. Give grownups a chance to share in your fun.

. . . Try to keep your space orderly as you work. Rinse each utensil and dispose of peelings and cans as you finish with them. It is lots more fun to serve and eat your masterpiece from a tidy kitchen.

. . . After you have practiced with several of the recipes, you will be ready to prepare and serve a real meal. Pages 67-72 offer menu-making and serving ideas. Read them carefully and decide whom you want to serve, what you'd like to cook, and when and where you will do it. Then check with the grownups to be sure your plans meet their approval. Invite your guests and make a shopping list. Remember, preparing the food, setting the table, and serving the food take time. Work out a timetable and get set to enjoy good food with good friends.

Cooking is an exciting way to learn and to grow creatively. I hope this little book will help you to do both.

Imogene Forte

BEVERAGES

MY RECIPES
Beverages

GRAPE JUICE FIZZLE

a delightful way to make grape juice sparkle

WHAT TO USE:

- quart jar or pitcher
- mixing spoon
- 4 glasses

- 2 cups clear soda
- 1 cup grape juice
- ice

WHAT TO DO:

1. Mix the soda and grape juice together.
2. Pour into glasses and add ice.

Serves 4

PEPPERMINT-ORANGE SQUISH

do-it-yourself vitamin C

WHAT TO USE:

- old-fashioned peppermint stick
- 1 navel orange

WHAT TO DO:

1. Hold the orange between the palms of your hands. Being very careful not to break it, roll and squeeze it until it begins to feel soft. Use your fingers to keep softening it.   **2.** When the orange feels *very* soft, stick the peppermint stick into it. **3.** Use the peppermint stick as a straw. Squeeze the orange gently as you drink and enjoy the peppermint–orange juice.

Serves 1

EGGNOG

an extra-special winter holiday treat

WHAT TO USE:

- mixing bowl
- egg beater
- measuring cup
- measuring spoon
- pretty cup

- 1 egg
- 2 teaspoons sugar
- salt
- 1 cup cold milk
- 1 teaspoon vanilla extract
- nutmeg

WHAT TO DO:

1. Break the egg into the mixing bowl and add the sugar and a pinch of salt.   **2.** Beat with the egg beater until frothy.   **3.** Add milk and vanilla extract.
4. Beat again with the egg beater.
5. Pour into the cup and sprinkle a little nutmeg on top.

Serves 1

ICE CREAM SODA

just like the soda shop special

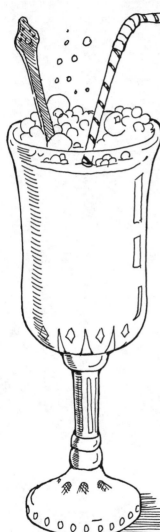

WHAT TO USE:

- tall glass
- spoon
- measuring spoon

- 3 tablespoons chocolate syrup
- 1 tablespoon milk
- 1 scoop ice cream (chocolate, vanilla, or other)
- soda water

WHAT TO DO:

1. Put the syrup and the milk into the glass.   **2.** Stir well.   **3.** Add the ice cream.   **4.** Fill the glass with soda water.   **5.** Stir again.   **6.** Insert a straw and enjoy!

Serves 1

FRIENDLY FRUIT PUNCH

for a festive summertime party

WHAT TO USE:

- large glass jar or pitcher
- mixing spoon

- orange, pineapple, and apple juices
- ginger ale
- ice

WHAT TO DO:

1. Pour the fruit juices into the jar or pitcher. **2.** Stir with the spoon. **3.** Put the jar or pitcher in the refrigerator to mix the flavors. **4.** Just before you serve the punch, add ginger ale and ice cubes.

Serves a crowd

PERFECT CHOCOLATE MILK

just the right thing for after-school hunger pangs

WHAT TO USE:

- tall glass
- mixing spoon
- measuring cup
- measuring spoon

- 1 cup milk
- 3 tablespoons chocolate syrup

WHAT TO DO:

1. Put the chocolate syrup and a little of the milk into the glass. **2.** Mix well. **3.** Add the rest of the milk, stirring as you pour.

Serves 1

FUDGY PUDGY SHAKE

a super weekend treat

WHAT TO DO:

1. Make Perfect Chocolate Milk (see page 18).   **2.** Add a scoop of chocolate or vanilla ice cream.   **3.** Put the chocolate milk and ice cream in a jar with a tightly fitting lid and shake until thick and frothy.   **4.** Serve with a straw and a spoon.

Serves 1

LUCKY LEMONADE

great for picnics

WHAT TO USE:

- tall glass
- sharp knife
- measuring spoon
- measuring cup
- spoon

- 1 lemon
- 2 tablespoons sugar
- 1 cup water
- ice

WHAT TO DO:

1. Use the knife to cut the lemon in half carefully.
2. Squeeze the lemon until you have 2 tablespoons of lemon juice.   **3.** Put it into the glass.   **4.** Add the sugar and stir well.   **5.** Pour the water into the glass and stir. Serve over ice.

Serves 1

LEMONADE BLUSH

guaranteed to cool you off on a warm summer day

WHAT TO DO:

1. Make Lucky Lemonade (see page 20).   **2.** Add a drop of red food coloring before you add the ice.   **3.** Stir, then add the ice.

Serves 1

SNACKS
and
SANDWICHES

MY RECIPES
Snacks and Sandwiches

BREAKFAST SMOOTHIE

a wake-me-up pick-me-up

WHAT TO USE:

- mixing bowls
- fork
- egg beater
- measuring cup
- measuring spoons

- 1 banana
- 1 egg
- 1 cup milk
- 1 teaspoon vanilla
- 1 teaspoon lemon juice
- 1 tablespoon molasses

WHAT TO DO:

1. Mash the banana with a fork in the mixing bowl.
2. Use the egg beater to beat the egg very well in a separate bowl. Add it to the banana.   **3.** Add the milk, vanilla, lemon juice and molasses.   **4.** Mix with egg beater until smooth.

Serves 1

FIVE-CUP HONEY-BUTTER BALLS

easy to measure, fun to make

WHAT TO USE:

- measuring cup
- large bowl
- wooden spoon
- waxed paper
- cookie sheet
- 1 cup honey
- 1 cup rice cereal
- 1 cup dry milk
- 1 cup peanut butter
- 1 cup coconut

WHAT TO DO:

1. Measure the honey, rice cereal, dry milk, and peanut butter into the bowl.   **2.** Stir with a wooden spoon until well mixed. **3.** Spread the coconut on waxed paper.   **4.** Shape the dough mixture into small balls and roll in the coconut until covered on all sides.   **5.** Place the balls on the cookie sheet.   **6.** Put in the refrigerator for half an hour or more before serving.

Serves the gang

CINNAMON-RAISIN SLICES

a morning treat or anytime snack

WHAT TO USE:

- mixing bowl
- mixing spoon
- knife
- measuring spoons
- measuring cup

- 6 slices raisin bread
- ¼ cup butter, softened
- 6 teaspoons sugar
- 1½ teaspoons cinnamon

WHAT TO DO:

1. Mix the cinnamon and sugar together in the mixing bowl. **2.** If you wish, you may toast the bread. **3.** Spread butter on the bread. **4.** Sprinkle cinnamon sugar mixture on the buttered bread slices.

Makes 6 slices

BANANA SURPRISE

a snack or treat

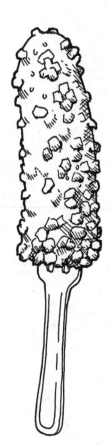

WHAT TO USE:

- rolling pin
- small bag
- knife
- plastic forks
- waxed paper
- measuring cups

- 1 banana
- ½ cup yogurt
- ¼ cup dry roasted peanuts

WHAT TO DO:

1. Crush the peanuts by putting them in a small bag and rolling them with the rolling pin.   **2.** Peel the banana and cut it in half.   **3.** Stick each half of the banana on a plastic fork.   **4.** Cover the banana halves with yogurt.   **5.** Spread the crushed peanuts on waxed paper. Roll the yogurt-covered banana pieces in the peanuts.   **6.** Take a bite. Ymmm!

Serves 2

SPROUTS IN A BLANKET

a healthy combination of tastes

WHAT TO USE:

- toothpicks
- serving plate
- knife
- colander

- lettuce leaves, rinsed and drained
- slices of corned beef, ham or roast beef
- your favorite cheese, sliced very thin or grated
- italian salad dressing
- alfalfa sprouts

WHAT TO DO:

1. Lay each lettuce leaf flat. **2.** Place a slice of meat and some cheese on top of the lettuce leaf. **3.** Sprinkle on some salad dressing. **4.** Add a handful of sprouts. **5.** Roll up the lettuce leaf and secure with a toothpick.

Serves as many as you wish

GREAT THINGS TO DO WITH PEANUT BUTTER

to make the world's greatest sandwiches

Mix PEANUT BUTTER with . . .

- ☐ applesauce and serve on cinnamon toast
- ☐ raisins and honey and serve on a bran muffin
- ☐ chopped pickles and spread on cheese crackers
- ☐ orange juice and grated orange rind and pile open-face on nut bread
- ☐ mashed bananas and spread on buttered raisin bread
- ☐ crushed peanuts and spread on toasted white bread strips

- [ ] coconut and crushed pineapple and spoon on a toasted english muffin half

- [ ] marshmallow cream and spread between vanilla wafers

- [ ] cream cheese and olives and spread on a bagel

- [ ] molasses and serve on graham crackers

- [ ] your favorite jam, jelly, or marmalade and serve on your choice of bread or crackers

Remember, peanut butter is loaded with vitamins and minerals that are good for the growing body.

SOME "GOOD ANYTIME" SNACKS THAT ARE GOOD FOR YOU

All of these treats are easy to fix and fun to eat. They taste every bit as good as junk food, and they are much better for your body.

Apple Slices. Wash an apple and cut it into 8 slices. Cut the seeds and core out of each slice. Sprinkle a little brown sugar and honey on the slices if you like.

Celery Stalks with Pimento Cheese. Wash a celery stalk, leaving the green leaves on. Fill the celery stalk with pimento cheese.

Nuts, Raisins, and Cereal. Put some nuts, raisins, and a handful of your favorite ready-to-eat cereal in a plastic bag. Shake the bag to mix them all up.

Bread and Butter Fingers. Cut a slice of bread into 3 fingers. Spread butter on the bread.

Carrot Curls. Wash a carrot. Use a knife to cut off thin strips. Put the strips in cold water and watch them curl.

Ham and Cheese on a Toothpick. Cut some good yellow cheese and a slice of ham into small cubes. Put a cube of cheese then a cube of ham, then another of each on a toothpick. Eat with crackers and pickles.

Berry Good Yogurt. Put some yogurt and strawberries or blueberries in a paper cup. Mix with a spoon and use the spoon to eat it!

Stuffed Dates. Split pitted dates across the top. Put a walnut and a dab of cream cheese into the opening and push the date back together.

Frosted Cucumber Circles. Wash a cucumber and cut off the ends. Slice the cucumber. Put cottage cheese between 2 circles to make little sandwiches.

Bananas and Vanilla Wafers. Peel a banana and slice it into pieces. Put each slice of banana between 2 vanilla wafers.

DIPS FOR CHIPS . . .

DILL DIP

WHAT TO USE:

- medium-size serving bowl
- mixing spoon
- measuring spoon
- 1 cup (8 oz.) dairy sour cream
- 1 tablespoon dill weed
- salt
- pepper

WHAT TO DO:

1. Place the sour cream and dill weed in the bowl. **2.** Mix well. **3.** Add salt and pepper to taste. **4.** Put it in the refrigerator for 30 minutes to thicken. **5.** Serve with crackers, melba toast, or corn chips.

Makes 1 cup

FRENCH ONION DIP

WHAT TO USE:

- medium-size serving bowl
- mixing spoon
- 1 cup (8 oz.) dairy sour cream
- 1 package dry onion soup mix

WHAT TO DO:

1. Place the sour cream and onion soup mix in the bowl. **2.** Mix well. **3.** Put it in the refrigerator for 30 minutes to thicken. **4.** Serve with corn chips or potato chips. Makes 1 cup

34

. . . and parties, snacks, and fingers!

BACON-TOMATO DIP

WHAT TO USE:

- medium-size serving bowl
- mixing spoon
- sharp knife
- measuring spoon

- 1 8-oz. package cream cheese, softened
- 1 cup (8 oz.) dairy sour cream
- 1 large tomato, washed and cut into small pieces
- 1 tablespoon dill weed
- 2 tablespoons bacon bits
- 1 tablespoon Worcestershire sauce

WHAT TO DO:

1. Place the cream cheese and sour cream in the bowl. **2.** Mix well. **3.** Add the pieces of tomato and mix again. **4.** Measure the dill weed, bacon bits, and Worcestershire sauce and blend into the mixture. **5.** Put it in the refrigerator for 30 minutes to thicken. **6.** Serve with different types of crackers.

Makes 2 cups

35

SALADS
and
MAIN DISHES

MY RECIPES

Salads and Main Dishes

COOL CUCUMBER AND CELERY SOUP

a fancy summer soup

WHAT TO USE:
- can opener
- large mixing bowl
- wire whisk
- paring knife
- cutting board
- glass jar with screw top
- 4 soup bowls
- 1 can cream of celery soup
- ½ soup can water
- ½ soup can sour cream
- 2 green onions
- 1 small cucumber
- celery leaves for garnish

WHAT TO DO:

1. Open the can of soup and put it in the bowl. **2.** Fill the soup can ½ full of water, then finish filling the can with sour cream. Dump the water and sour cream in the bowl with the soup. **3.** Use the wire whisk to mix the soup, water, and sour cream until all the lumps are gone. **4.** Peel the cucumber and onions and chop them into very small pieces. Mix them into the soup. **5.** Pour the mixture into a glass jar with a screw top. Put the jar in the refrigerator and leave it for several hours to let the flavors blend. **6.** When ready to serve, shake the jar before pouring the soup into the soup bowls (glass ones, if you have them). **7.** Put some celery leaves in the middle of each soup bowl. Serves 4

VEGETABLES AND CHEESE IN PITA BREAD

a pocketful of goodies

WHAT TO USE:

- knife
- cutting board
- measuring spoon
- measuring cup
- 2 tomatoes
- 1 bell pepper
- 1 cup sprouts
- 1 avocado
- 1 small onion
- 1 cucumber
- 2 tablespoons french or italian dressing
- 4 slices swiss cheese
- 4 pieces of pita bread

WHAT TO DO:

1. Wash the tomatoes and pepper. Peel the onion, avocado, and cucumber. **2.** Cut the tomatoes, pepper, onion, avocado, and cucumber into bite-size pieces. Place a sufficient amount in each pita bread pocket. **3.** Add ¼ cup sprouts and a cheese slice. **4.** Measure and add ½ tablespoon dressing to each serving.

Serves 4

ORANGE-AVOCADO SALAD

a delightfully different salad

WHAT TO USE:
- knife
- large bowl
- measuring cups
- salad dressing bottle with lid
- measuring spoons
- serving plates
- colander
- 1 avocado
- 2 oranges
- 2 cups alfalfa sprouts
- ½ cup nuts
- 5 tablespoons oil
- 3 tablespoons lemon juice
- 2 tablespoons sweet pickle relish
- ½ teaspoon sugar
- ½ teaspoon salt
- ¼ teaspoon black pepper
- lettuce leaves, washed and drained

WHAT TO DO:
1. Slice and peel the avocado.   **2.** Peel the oranges and tear the sections apart. Take out the seeds.   **3.** Put the sprouts, orange sections, nuts, and avocado slices in the bowl.   **4.** Measure the oil, lemon juice, pickle relish, sugar, salt, and pepper into the bottle and shake it all together.   **5.** Pour the dressing over the salad and stir it all together.   **6.** Serve the orange-avocado salad on lettuce leaves.

GOOD-FOR-YOU CARROT SALAD

bunnies' most requested dish

WHAT TO USE:
- grater
- knife
- measuring spoons
- mixing spoon
- salad bowl
- measuring cups
- colander
- 2 carrots
- ½ cup raisins
- 2 apples
- 2 stalks celery
- ½ cup nuts
- 1 cup mayonnaise
- ¼ teaspoon salt
- ¼ teaspoon sugar
- 1 teaspoon lemon juice
- lettuce leaves, washed and drained

WHAT TO DO:

1. Wash the carrots, apples, and celery. **2.** Grate the carrots into the salad bowl. Add the raisins. **3.** Chop the apples, celery, and nuts and add them to the carrots and raisins. **4.** Measure the mayonnaise, salt, sugar, and lemon juice and add them to the mixture in the bowl. **5.** Mix well. **6.** Serve on lettuce leaves. Sprinkle some extra raisins and nuts on top of each serving if you wish.

Serves 6

TUNA TAKEOVERS

for all fish-lovers and friends

WHAT TO USE:

- can opener
- strainer
- knife
- mixing bowl
- mixing spoon
- measuring cup
- measuring spoon

- 1 small can tuna
- ¼ cup mayonnaise
- 2 stalks celery
- ¼ cup pickle relish
- 1 tablespoon lemon juice
- 4 small, soft rolls

WHAT TO DO:

1. Drain the tuna and empty it into the bowl.   **2.** Wash the celery, then chop it.   **3.** Add the celery, mayonnaise, lemon juice, and pickle relish to the tuna. **4.** Stir until well mixed.   **5.** Split the rolls and fill them with the tuna mixture.

Serves 4

MEAT-AND-CHEESE ROLL-UPS

(or meat-and-cheese party platter)

WHAT TO USE:
- platter
- knife
- mixing bowl
- measuring spoons
- 6 slices roast beef
- 6 thin slices swiss cheese
- 6 small sweet pickles
- 1 small jar pimento cheese spread
- 6 thin slices ham
- 6 slices bologna
- 1 8-oz. package cream cheese, softened
- 2 tablespoons mayonnaise
- 1 teaspoon lemon juice
- 6 green olives
- extra pickles and olives

WHAT TO DO:
(for beef-and-swiss roll-ups) **1.** Spread the roast beef slices flat. **2.** Place a swiss cheese slice on top of each beef slice. **3.** Place a pickle on one edge of the meat and cheese. **4.** Roll the meat and cheese around the pickle. **5.** Place the roll on the platter with the edge down.

(for bologna-and-cream cheese roll-ups)
1. Put the cream cheese in a bowl. **2.** Add
the mayonnaise and lemon juice. **3.** Chop
the olives and add them to the cheese.
4. Spread the bologna slices flat. **5.** Cover
each bologna slice with cream cheese.
6. Roll up and put on the platter. Add some
extra pickles and olives to the platter and
serve.

(for ham-and-pimento roll-ups) **1.** Spread
the ham slices flat. **2.** Cover each ham
slice with pimento cheese. **3.** Roll the ham
slice up and place on the platter.

Makes 18 roll-ups

NUTTY BANANA SALAD

good for a birthday celebration

WHAT TO USE:
- knife
- small bowl
- waxed paper
- measuring cup
- measuring spoon
- mixing spoon
- 2 salad plates
- colander
- 2 lettuce leaves, washed and drained
- 2 tablespoons mayonnaise
- 2 tablespoons sugar
- 2 bananas
- 1 cup crushed peanuts
- 2 maraschino cherries

WHAT TO DO:
1. Cut each banana into 6 pieces. **2.** Mix the mayonnaise and sugar together in the bowl. **3.** Use the knife to spread mayonnaise mixture on all sides of the banana pieces. **4.** Spread the crushed peanuts on the waxed paper. **5.** Roll the banana pieces in peanuts until they are completely covered. **6.** Place a lettuce leaf on each salad plate, and put 6 of the nutty banana pieces on each lettuce leaf. **7.** Top each salad with a cherry and serve.

Serves 2

SWEET CLOUDS 'N FRUIT

a billowy, tasty treat for a crowd

WHAT TO USE:

- large, attractive serving bowl
- large mixing bowl
- mixing spoon
- can opener
- knife

- 1 1-lb. container cottage cheese (small curd)
- 1 3-oz. box orange gelatin
- 1 small can crushed pineapple, drained well
- 1 can mandarin oranges or fruit cocktail, drained
- 2 or 3 bananas, sliced
- other canned or fresh fruit in season (peaches, grapes, apricots, cherries)
- large container frozen nondairy whipped topping

WHAT TO DO:

1. Combine cottage cheese and gelatin. **2.** Mix well.
3. Add drained canned and fresh fruit.   **4.** Carefully fold in whipped topping. **5.** Turn in to serving bowl and refrigerate until serving time.

Serves 12

GARBANZO BEAN SALAD

a great lunch!

WHAT TO USE:
- cutting board
- knife
- wooden spoon
- mixing spoon
- salad bowl
- colander
- 1 small can garbanzo beans (chick peas)
- 2 green onions
- 3 pimentos
- 2 stalks celery
- ¼ teaspoon sugar
- 2 tablespoons mayonnaise
- lettuce leaves, washed and drained

WHAT TO DO:
1. Wash the onions and celery.   **2.** Drain the garbanzo beans and put them into the salad bowl.   **3.** Chop the onions (tops and all), celery, and 2 pimentos. Add them to the beans. **4.** Measure the sugar and mayonnaise and add them to the beans and vegetables.   **5.** Mix well with the wooden spoon.   **6.** Push the mixture away from the sides of the bowl. Place lettuce leaves around the side of the bowl. **7.** Cut 1 pimento into strips to place in center of salad for garnish.   **8.** Serve and enjoy!

Serves 4

PINEAPPLE-PIMENTO CHEESE SALAD

cheese and fruit are buddies

WHAT TO USE:
- large mixing bowl
- wooden spoon
- can opener
- salad plates
- colander
- measuring cups
- 1 jar pimento cheese spread
- 1 small container nondairy whipped topping
- 1 small can crushed pineapple (with juice)
- 1 cup miniature marshmallows
- ½ cup broken nut meats
- lettuce leaves, washed and drained

WHAT TO DO:
1. Put the pimento cheese and nondairy topping in a large bowl. Mix well.
2. Open the can of pineapple and dump it into the mixing bowl. Stir until well mixed.   **3.** Fold the marshmallows and nuts into the mixture. **4.** Put the bowl in the refrigerator for about one hour.   **5.** Place lettuce leaves on salad plates and top each with a big spoonful of pineapple-cheese mix. (You can add a little mayonnaise and a nut to each salad if you like.)
Serves 6

DESSERTS
and
SPECIAL TREATS

MY RECIPES
Desserts and Special Treats

INDIVIDUAL BOSTON CREAM PIES

for you and a special friend

WHAT TO USE:

- 2 plates
- sharp knife
- spoon
- measuring cup
- glass jar with tightly fitting lid

- 2 cake doughnuts (unglazed)
- 1 small box instant vanilla pudding mix
- 2 cups milk
- chocolate syrup

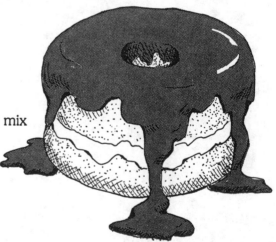

WHAT TO DO:

1. Mix pudding and milk in glass jar.   **2.** Shake until well mixed and firm.
3. Carefully slice doughnuts in half. Place one bottom half on each plate. Set the top halves aside.   **4.** Spoon vanilla pudding onto each bottom half. Replace the top halves.   **5.** Drizzle chocolate syrup over filled "pies."   **6.** Put in the refrigerator until serving time.

Serves 2

FRESH FRUIT PARFAIT

a striped dessert

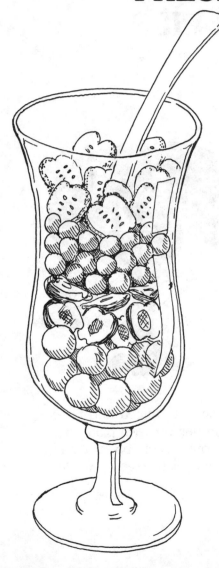

WHAT TO USE:

- colander
- spoon
- knife
- parfait glasses

- seedless grapes
- cherries
- blueberries
- strawberries

WHAT TO DO:

1. Wash and drain the fruit, keeping the different kinds of fruit separated.   **2.** Cut the cherries in half and remove the pits.   **3.** Slice the strawberries.   **4.** In each parfait glass, place a few grapes, then some cherries, then blueberries, then strawberries on top. Don't mix the fruits — let them stay in layers. That's what makes the parfait!

Servings vary according to the amount of fruit used

54

PEPPERMINT WONDERS

use appropriate food coloring for special holidays

WHAT TO USE:
- sifter
- waxed paper
- measuring cups
- measuring spoon
- mixing bowl
- mixing spoon
- fork
- 4 cups sifted powdered sugar
- ⅔ cup sweetened condensed milk
- ¼ teaspoon peppermint flavoring
- food coloring

WHAT TO DO:

1. Sift the sugar onto waxed paper. Measure 4 cups. **2.** Mix the milk and peppermint flavoring in the mixing bowl. **3.** Add 3 drops of food coloring and mix again. **4.** Gradually beat in the sugar. **5.** Mix well, then work the mixture with your hands until it is smooth and stiff. **6.** Pinch off small pieces and form into approximately 30 balls. **7.** Place the mints on waxed paper and press them gently with the back of a fork.

Makes 30

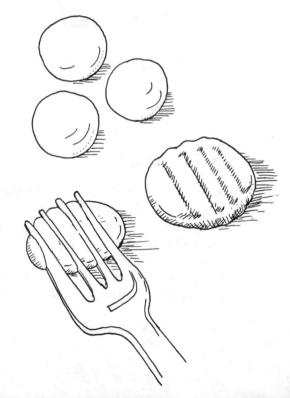

MINT CRUNCH SURPRISE

all the favorites — chocolate, mint, ice cream

WHAT TO USE:

- spoon
- 1 pint chocolate chip ice cream, softened
- 1 pint mint chocolate chip ice cream, softened
- 1 9-in. prepared chocolate cookie crumb crust
- chocolate chips or nuts, if you wish

WHAT TO DO:

1. Set out the chocolate chip ice cream to soften. Pack it into the pie crust smoothly and evenly.   **2.** Put it into the freezer for an hour.   **3.** While it is in the freezer, let the mint chocolate chip ice cream soften.   **4.** Remove the pie from the freezer and pack the mint chocolate chip ice cream on top of the chocolate chip ice cream.   **5.** Put the pie back into the freezer for another hour.   **6.** Take the pie out of the freezer 20 minutes before you plan to serve it. **7.** Decorate the top of the pie with chocolate chips or nuts, if you wish.

Makes 1 delicious pie

CHERRY DREAM CUPS

the grand finale for your most elegant dinner

WHAT TO USE:

- 2 mixing bowls
- egg beater
- wooden spoon
- measuring spoons
- measuring cup
- muffin tin with 10 paper baking cups in place
- serving plates or bowl
- 2 egg whites (see page 76 to learn how to separate an egg)
- 2 tablespoons sugar
- ½ pint cream
- ⅓ cup maraschino cherries, drained (save the juice) and chopped
- 2 tablespoons maraschino cherry juice
- ⅓ cup Grape Nuts cereal
- 1 teaspoon almond flavoring

WHAT TO DO:

1. In one bowl, use the egg beater to beat the egg whites until stiff.   **2.** Beat in the sugar.   **3.** In the other bowl, whip the cream until it forms peaks. **4.** Combine the contents of the 2 bowls.   **5.** Fold in the maraschino cherries, cherry juice, Grape Nuts, and almond flavoring.   **6.** Mix gently and spoon into the baking cups.   **7.** Put in the freezer overnight. When ready to serve, place each baking cup upside down on a serving plate and peel off the paper. Serves 10

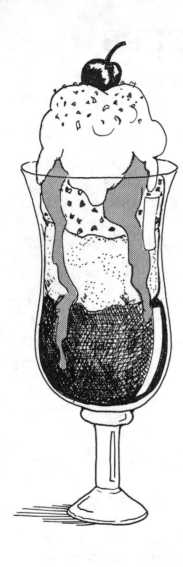

SUPER SUNDAE

as simple or elaborate as you want

WHAT TO USE:

- large dish
- ice cream scoop or large spoon

- ice cream (one or more flavors)
- toppings (see below)

WHAT TO DO:

1. Dip the spoon or scoop in hot water before you use it so it will be easier to scoop the ice cream.   **2.** Place 2 or 3 scoops of your favorite flavors in the dish.   **3.** Add one or more of the following toppings and garnishes.

Toppings	*Garnishes*
chocolate syrup	whipped cream
honey	chopped nuts
maple syrup	coconut
jam	crushed cookies
fresh or canned fruit	maraschino cherries
butterscotch	jimmies

NO-COOK S'MORES

for days and nights when there's no handy campfire

WHAT TO USE:

- table knife

- graham crackers
- marshmallow cream
- 1 can ready-to-spread milk chocolate frosting

WHAT TO DO:

1. For each s'more, spread 1 graham cracker square with a thick layer of chocolate frosting.   **2.** Spread the second square with marshmallow cream. **3.** Put together sandwich-style with the frosting and marshmallow cream on the inside.

STRAWBERRY SHORTCAKE

an old-fashioned favorite

WHAT TO USE:

- 6 individual serving dishes
- spoon
- measuring cup
- 1 plain pound cake from bakery or grocery store
- 2 cups sliced fresh or frozen strawberries (sprinkle fresh strawberries with sugar, if desired)
- small container nondairy whipped topping
- 6 whole strawberries for garnish

WHAT TO DO:

1. Cut 6 slices of pound cake and place on dishes. **2.** Spoon strawberries generously over cake and top with whipped topping. **3.** Garnish each serving with a whole strawberry and serve immediately.

Serves 6

RASPBERRY DELIGHT WITH FRUIT

colorful and festive!

WHAT TO USE:

- colander
- large spoon or ice cream scoop
- serving bowls or plates

- 1 pint raspberry sherbet
- seedless grapes
- strawberries
- plain cookies, if you wish

WHAT TO DO:

1. Wash and drain grapes and strawberries.
2. Working quickly, scoop raspberry sherbet into bowls or onto plates.   **3.** Add grapes and strawberries attractively around sherbet.
4. Serve with a cookie if you wish.

Serves 6 or 8

FRUITY CHEESE BOARD

the perfect ending to a special dinner

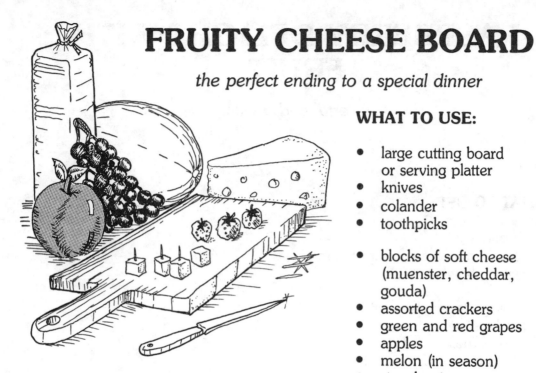

WHAT TO USE:

- large cutting board or serving platter
- knives
- colander
- toothpicks

- blocks of soft cheese (muenster, cheddar, gouda)
- assorted crackers
- green and red grapes
- apples
- melon (in season)
- strawberries

WHAT TO DO:

1. Wash and drain the fruit.   **2.** Core and slice the apples.   **3.** Cut the melon in half and remove the seeds. Cut each half into wedges.   **4.** Arrange the fruit, cheese, and crackers on the board or platter. Place 2 or 3 knives on the board. **5.** Use toothpicks to spear the fruit and cheese.

Servings vary according to amount of fruit and cheese

ICE CREAM SANDWICH

use the flavors and cookies you like

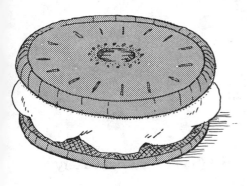

WHAT TO USE:

- large spoon

- ice cream, slightly softened
- large cookies

WHAT TO DO:

1. Place a scoop of ice cream in the center of one cookie.   **2.** Place another cookie on top, squash it down, and enjoy!   **3.** Don't forget to make one for a friend.

WHIPPED CREAM TUNNEL CAKE

everyone will ask how you did it — don't tell!

WHAT TO USE:

- large mixing bowl
- egg beater
- sharp knife
- measuring cups
- mixing spoon
- cake plate
- measuring spoon
- 1 prepared angel food cake from bakery or grocery store
- 1 pint heavy whipping cream
- 1 cup sliced fresh or well-drained frozen strawberries
- 1 cup toasted slivered almonds
- ⅓ cup confectioner's sugar
- 8 whole strawberries

WHAT TO DO:

1. Place cake on cake plate.   **2.** Using the sharp knife, carefully and evenly cut off the top inch of cake and set it aside (figure A).   **3.** Create a "tunnel" by inserting the knife 1 inch from the outer edge of the cake and piercing about 1½ inch down through it (figure B).   **4.** Carefully continue slicing all the way around the outside edge, being careful not to cut through the bottom.   **5.** Repeat this process 1 inch from inside edge.   **6.** Using a fork, carefully remove the center section (figure C).   **7.** To prepare the filling, whip the cream with the egg beater

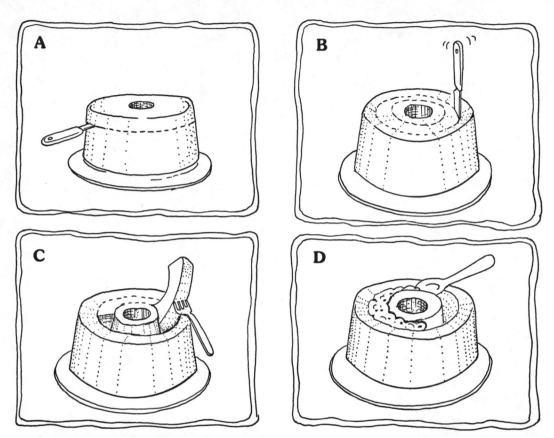

until it is stiff. **8.** Slowly add the confectioner's sugar a tablespoon at a time, beating after each addition. **9.** Gently fold in the almonds and strawberries. **10.** Spoon the mixture into the "tunnel" and pack lightly, making sure the tunnel is filled but not overflowing (figure D). **11.** Replace the top of the cake and use the remaining mixture to frost it. **12.** Decorate with whole strawberries and serve immediately to people you like.

Makes 1 cake

SERVING IN STYLE

Be sure that you take time to serve your food in a nice way. It will taste better and be more of a treat for you and your guests. If you can, use your prettiest dishes, glasses, flatware, and linens.

Follow this example to set the table correctly.

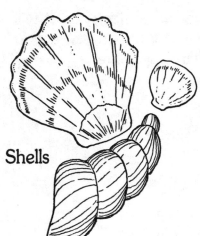

Planning special centerpieces or decorations will be fun too. Try to think of themes, then look around for some unusual things to use. Flowers, plants and fruits are always nice, but why not try some other creative ideas of your own . . .

Shells

A bird's nest with a tiny artificial bird

Paper hearts or shamrocks

Small stuffed toys

Your food may
be served
buffet-style
or on a tray.

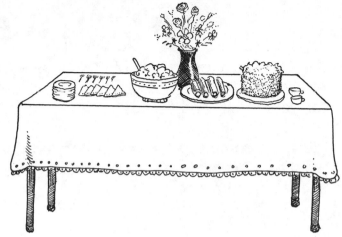

You might even want to try a more informal
setting, such as hobo- or picnic-style.

MENU MAKERS

After you have tried some of the no-cook, cook & learn recipes, you will be ready to plan and prepare special meals, snacks or party treats for your family and friends.

Here are some suggestions to help you get started. Later you will want to select other recipes and add some of your own to make your special menu magic.

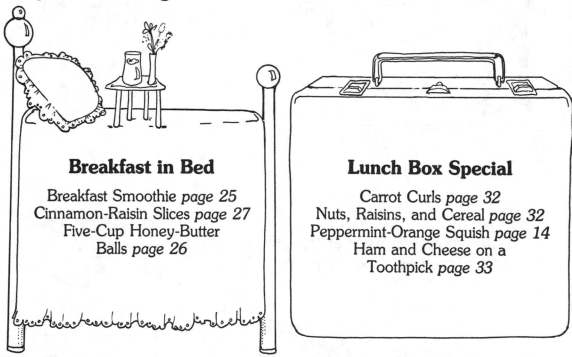

Breakfast in Bed

Breakfast Smoothie *page 25*
Cinnamon-Raisin Slices *page 27*
Five-Cup Honey-Butter
Balls *page 26*

Lunch Box Special

Carrot Curls *page 32*
Nuts, Raisins, and Cereal *page 32*
Peppermint-Orange Squish *page 14*
Ham and Cheese on a
Toothpick *page 33*

Surprise-the-Family Lunch

Sweet Clouds 'N Fruit *page 47*
Tuna Takeovers *page 43*
Grape Juice Fizzle *page 13*
Mint Crunch Surprise *page 56*

Company Dinner

Cool Cucumber and Celery Soup
page 39
Stuffed Dates *page 33*
Good-for-You Carrot Salad *page 42*
Sprouts in a Blanket *page 29*
Cherry Dream Cups *page 57*
Lemonade Blush *page 21*

Holiday or Birthday Brunch

Bread and Butter Fingers *page 32*
Orange-Avocado Salad *page 41*
Meat-and-Cheese Roll-ups *page 44*
Whipped Cream Tunnel Cake *page 64*
Eggnog *page 15*

Picnic in the Park

Vegetables and Cheese in Pita Bread *page 40*
Apple Slices *page 32*
Lucky Lemonade *page 20*
No-Cook S'mores *page 59*

GLOSSARY

BEAT: Stir mixture quickly and hard.

BLEND: Mix ingredients until smooth.

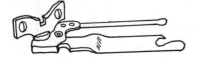

CAN OPENER: Utensil used to open bottles and tin cans.

CHOP: Cut into small pieces.

COLANDER: Drainer used to remove excess liquid from large foods.

DRAIN: Pour off liquid or place food in colander or strainer until liquid is gone.

DRIZZLE: Slowly pour one ingredient over the food.

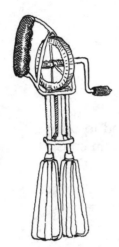

EGG BEATER: A rotary utensil that mixes liquid ingredients together or adds air to cream or egg whites.

FOLD: Gently mix ingredients by bringing spoon through the center, along the bottom, and up and over again.

FROTHY: Foaming or bubbly.

GARNISH: Add something extra to make the food more attractive.

GRATE: Shred ingredients into small pieces.

GRATER: Utensil used to shred cheese, fruit, and vegetables.

KNIFE: Utensil used to cut, slice, or chop.

MEASURING CUPS:
One cup or 4 individual cups, divided into 4 measurements: ¼ cup, ⅓ cup, ½ cup, 1 cup.

MEASURING SPOONS: Usually a set of 4 spoons, divided into 4 measurements: ¼ teaspoon, ½ teaspoon, 1 teaspoon, 1 tablespoon. 3 teaspoons equal 1 tablespoon.

MIX: Stir ingredients together.

MIXING BOWLS AND MIXING SPOONS:
Used to mix, beat, and combine ingredients.

PARFAIT:
Layers of ingredients placed attractively on top of each other.

PEEL: Take off outer covering.

SEPARATING AN EGG: You need an egg and 2 small bowls. Carefully crack the egg on the edge of one of the bowls. Pull the 2 halves apart, letting the clear part (the egg white) fall into one of the bowls. Carefully transfer the yellow part (the yolk) from one half to the other a few times so all the egg white will be separated. Try not to break the yolk. Put the yolk in the second bowl. See **beaten egg whites,** page 77.

SIEVE OR STRAINER:
Used to drain excess liquid off small foods.

SIFTER: Used to mix different dry ingredients together or to break dry ingredients into finer particles.

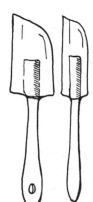

SPATULA: A rubber or plastic utensil used to fold, stir, or to scrape a bowl.

TOSS: Mix ingredients lightly.

WHIP: Add air by beating very quickly.

WHIPPED CREAM or BEATEN EGG WHITES:

Use the wire whisk or egg beater to beat the cream or egg white until it begins to get thick. Lift the whisk or egg beater from the mixture. If the mixture forms a little peak that doesn't keep standing up, it is a **soft peak.** If you want it to be a **stiff peak,** keep beating until the peak stands up stiffly.

WIRE WHISK: A utensil used to add air to liquid ingredients.

INDEX